40 Years of Buses
in
NEWCASTLE UPON TYNE

BY

G. Eric Hutchinson FCIT

Venture *publications*

Above: Newcastle Corporation fleet No. 325 (NVK 325), a 1950 AEC Regent III with Northern Coachbuilders bodywork, at Gosforth Park terminus in 1969.

Front cover: Busways fleet No. 907 (F907 JRG), one of 38 Alexander-bodied Scania N113 saloons in the fleet, at Grainger Street on 24th May 1989.

PHOTOGRAPHY

The majority of the photographs used in this book were taken by David Little between 1968 and 1995. Other pictures were supplied by:

Robert C. Davis	2, 7, 8 (upper and lower right), 9, 13 (upper), 16, 17 (upper), 18, 19, 20 (lower), 22, 23, 24 (upper), 33 (lower), 48 (lower), 56, 79 (upper).
Photobus/R. Marshall	8 (upper left), 11 (lower), 12 (upper)
Photobus/R. L. Kell	11 (upper), 15 (upper)
Photobus/A. Douglas	14
Photobus/G. Morant	21 (upper left and right) 24 (lower)
Photobus/ A. Richardson	12 (lower), 13 (lower), 15 (lower), 40 (upper).
Mark Hughes	Map
G. E. Hutchinson	63 (lower) 70 (upper), 73 (lower left), 75, 80 (lower both)
G. E. Hutchinson collection	20 (upper), 31, 64 (lower)

CONTENTS

Introduction	3
Historical information	6
Part One 1956-1969	
Newcastle Corporation	7
Northern General Transport and Associated Companies	11
United Automobile Services	18
Ribble Motor Services	19
Venture Transport	20
O.K. Motor Services	21
Other independent operators	22
Part Two 1970-1986	
Tyneside/Tyne and Wear PTE	25
Northern General Transport and Associated Companies	34
United Automobile Services	48
Ribble Motor Services	48
Scottish Omnibuses	51
Venture Transport	56
O.K. Motor Services	57
Other independent operators	58
Part Three 1986-1996	
Busways Travel Services	60
Tyne & Wear Omnibus Company	66
Welcome Passenger Services	66
Go Ahead Group	67
O.K. Motor Services	71
Northumbria Motor Services	72
Cumberland Motor Services	74
United Automobile Services	75
Tees & District Transport	75
Other operators	76

ISBN 1 898432 72 4 © G. E. HUTCHINSON MAY 1996

COMPUTERISED PRODUCTION FOR THE PUBLISHERS BY MOPOK GRAPHICS 128 PIKES LANE, GLOSSOP, DERBYSHIRE.

Introduction

The City of Newcastle upon Tyne is the 'regional capital' of the north east of England and its citizens have for long been served by innovative and extensive local transport systems. In earlier years local railway lines and extensive tramway and trolleybus systems played a major role. Of course since 1979 the Tyne and Wear Metro has been a key feature. This book is devoted mainly to motor buses and in particular the last 40 years. The Newcastle trolleybus system is covered too and it played an important role until its closure in 1966.

At this stage it is interesting to note that over the 40 years covered by this book and even earlier, there was never a single dominant bus operator providing services within, to and from Newcastle. For most of the time there have always been at least three large operators as well as the smaller operators. Consequently, because many roads have been served by more than one of the large operators there has always been a level of competition and choice for passengers perhaps not apparent in some other towns and cities. The buses referred to in this book are therefore not just those running wholly within the city, but also those on the extensive services to and from the city. Long distance express type services have not been covered in this book as I felt that the space I had available should be devoted to the almost never ending variety of buses serving local journey needs. To this end the book covers buses which could be seen in the heart of the city and this area is shown on the map on page 5.

Motor bus services started in the city in 1912 with the first Newcastle Corporation buses running between Fenham Barracks, Westerhope and Whorlton Church. After the First World War developments were rapid and by the late 1920s a number of large and many smaller operators had become well established. The 1930 Road Traffic Act introduced licences for services and higher standards of vehicle

fitness and in many ways a process was started which created the framework which was still in place in the first period reviewed in this book.

I have divided this book into three periods – 1956 to 1969, 1970 to 1986 and 1986 to 1996. In this first period local services within the city were almost exclusively provided by Newcastle Corporation. However, some of these were part of an extensive network of services to and from Gateshead via the High Level and Tyne bridges operated jointly with the Gateshead and District Omnibus Company, an associated company of British Electric Traction owned Northern General Transport. Newcastle Corporation also provided joint services with three other Northern General associated companies – Tyneside Tramways and Tramroads Company on a service between Croft Street and Wallsend and Tynemouth and District Transport Company and Wakefield's Motors on a service between Haymarket and Tynemouth via the Coast Road. However, for many local citizens the yellow and cream liveried fleet of the Corporation was the predominant means of transport within the city. However, a much different position existed for journeys to and from the city. Extensive services were provided by Northern General and its associated company Sunderland District, by the state-owned United Automobile Services, by the 95 vehicle independent Venture Transport and by a number of smaller independent operators also. Although the pattern of services provided by these companies was substantial there was a degree of logic about it. Northern General and Sunderland District linked the city with large parts of the north and mid County Durham including Hebburn, Jarrow, South Shields, Sunderland and Wearside and points further south such as Hartlepool, Middlesbrough, Stockton and Darlington. These longer distance routes were worked jointly with United as a result of territorial agreements made in the 1920s. United also linked the city with north, mid and south east Northumberland (some services jointly with Scottish Omnibuses) and also the Tyne valley projecting west as

far as Hexham, Allendale and Allenheads as well as the lengthy service to Carlisle. United was also involved in joint working with Tynemouth and District Transport Company on a service between Haymarket and Whitley Bay via the Coast Road and this was coordinated with the Newcastle Corporation/Tynemouth and District/Wakefield's service between Haymarket and Tynemouth via the Coast Road referred to earlier giving a five minute frequency between Haymarket and Billy Mill near North Shields. Venture Transport linked the city with north west County Durham and its services were to some extent coordinated with Northern General (from Consett) and United (in the Tyne valley). There was also a pattern to the use of the three main bus stations used by services to and from the city. Worswick Street, owned by Northern General, was used by services from north and mid County Durham and points further south as well as south Tyneside and Wearside. Marlborough Crescent, owned by the City Council, was used by services from north west County Durham, the Tyne valley and some longer distance services from south west County Durham. Haymarket, also owned by the City Council, was used by services from Northumberland. Taken together these three bus stations were extremely busy and certainly over-crowded at peak travel times. A further noticeable feature of many of the services operating to and from the city was the use of single-deck buses necessitated by the many low railway bridges in the mining areas of County Durham and Northumberland. Thus duplicate buses were used extensively on these very busy services.

A major change in March 1968 was the completion of the sale of the British Electric Traction Company's road passenger transport interests to the state-owned Transport Holding Company. This was a foretaste of things to come in that it had become apparent that calls for greater coordination or integration of public transport services would eventually be facilitated. This was brought about by the 1968 Transport Act which amongst other provisions established, from 1st January 1969, the National Bus Company (NBC) bringing together United and Northern General and its subsidiaries in single ownership. However, of even more significance for buses in Newcastle was the establishment of the Tyneside Passenger Transport Authority (PTA) and Executive (PTE). The PTE took ownership of Newcastle Corporation's buses from 1st January 1970.

In the second period covered by this book, from 1970 to 1986, buses in Newcastle were set for major change as the principal purpose of the PTA/PTE structure was 'to secure or promote the provision of a properly integrated and efficient system of public passenger transport to meet the needs of the area'. The PTE was given power to co-operate with other public transport providers, particularly British Rail and the National Bus Company, in furtherance of its principal purpose. An early development, no doubt prompted by the establishment of the PTA and PTE, was the sale of Venture Transport to Northern General in April 1970. The PTE pursued its integration responsibilities with vigour and there was an increasingly obvious impact on the city's bus services, including integration with the Metro system which was opened in phases between 1979 and 1983. The PTE and NBC subsidiaries cooperated within the terms of agreements made between them and this resulted in substantial changes to bus routes to 'feed' the Metro system including through-ticketing systems. Associated publicity material was issued for the complete system to inform potential passengers in a clear and concise fashion. PTE buses retained the yellow and cream livery which was for a period simplified and then replaced by a brighter yellow and white scheme. Buses of the NBC subsidiaries operating on services wholly within the Passenger Transport Area were gradually painted into a yellow version of the standard NBC livery and this was later superseded by an identical livery to

PTE buses including 'Tyne and Wear Transport' fleetnames. Also, by the end of 1975 all of the Northern General subsidiaries had ceased trading and all operations were then by that company itself. The bus service changes associated with Metro integration had the greatest impact on the services to and from the city operated by Northern General although services operated by PTE buses and United were also affected. The agreements between the PTE and the NBC subsidiaries provided for agreed mileage proportions to be operated by PTE buses, Northern General and United and so there were service reallocations between operators and depots as the phased introduction of Metro and integrated bus services proceeded. As there were less bus services directly into the city from Metro-served areas, the use of some bus stations reduced. This was particularly apparent at Worswick Street. In addition the City Council had developed a new bus station in the major Eldon Square shopping development in the north of the city centre. To meet obvious passenger needs many Northern General and United services were extended to Eldon Square from Marlborough Crescent whose use declined substantially. In this period OK Motor Services also moved its long-established Bishop Auckland service from Marlborough Crescent to a newly-created bus stand in Newgate Street, also adjacent to the Eldon Square shopping development. Inevitably the many changes associated with the integration of bus and Metro services were controversial. Although official and unofficial observers regarded the scheme as a success there were adjustments made in the light of experience which resulted in the re-introduction of some through bus services to the city on Metro-served corridors to give an element of choice. However, this was not before the successful road service licence application by Low Fell Coaches to provide a cross Tyne bus service between Low Fell, Gateshead and Newcastle.

By the mid-1980s it was clear that the bus operators were going to experience further change arising from the 1985 Transport Act. This had three principal purposes – to deregulate the operation of bus services, to revise bus service subsidy arrangements by

introducing a tendering system and to enable the privatisation of publicly-owned bus companies. Thus buses in Newcastle were again set to enter a new period.

The period 1986-1996 was just as eventful as the previous sixteen years. In the lead up to deregulation the three major operators in Newcastle changed their identities. PTE Buses, as it by then called itself, became Busways Travel Services which was owned by Tyne and Wear PTA and traded in Newcastle as City Busways and Newcastle Busways with yellow, maroon and white liveries and Blue Bus Services (blue and cream). Northern General became Go Ahead Northern with a new red and white livery which very quickly replaced the yellow livery and standard NBC red livery used previously on its vehicles. United was split into a number of parts and the main replacement in Newcastle was Northumbria Motor Services which adopted an elaborate red, grey and white livery. However, buses of the remaining smaller United and its offshoot Tees and District could still be seen entering Newcastle from South Durham and Cleveland, mainly on routes joint with Go Ahead Northern. Very soon privatisation took place with Go Ahead Northern and Northumbria being purchased from NBC by their senior management teams in 1987. Busways was purchased from Tyne and Wear PTA by its senior management and employees in 1989 with the employees receiving their shares through an employee share ownership plan (ESOP). Of the smaller operators OK Motor Services, which now presented itself as OK Travel, grew rapidly through success in the tendering process and the eventual conversion of many of these routes to commercial, non-subsidised, operation. Indeed OK Travel grew in this period from a fleet of 80 vehicles in 1986 to 225 vehicles in 1995. Of the other smaller operators serving Newcastle prior to 1986, Vasey and Low Fell Coaches continued initially much as before although Vasey competed with Blue Bus Services between Ponteland and Newcastle for a period. However deregulation brought a number of new operators to Newcastle and probably the most high profile example was the Tyne & Wear Omnibus Company (TWOC) which was in the same ownership as the long-established Trimdon Motor Services in County Durham. Tyne & Wear Omnibus Company commenced as a 20-vehicle operation in Newcastle in 1987 and grew to a fleet of 88 vehicles serving Newcastle and Sunderland by late 1989 when it was sold initially to Go Ahead Northern and then on the same day resold to Busways. The fleet was mainly elderly Bristol LH saloons in a blue and white livery and services were provided on some of Busways busiest routes in the city. A further high profile operator, Welcome Passenger Services, commenced services against Busways in 1991 using a fleet of 21 new MCW and Renault minibuses and this grew to a fleet of 38 minibuses by the time of its acquisition by Busways in 1993. Welcome initially used a livery and route numbers almost identical to Busways but these were modified after a legal challenge by Busways on these aspects. Go Ahead Northern commenced a restructuring in 1991 which resulted in new subsidiary companies taking over operations from the parent company. This soon brought five new identities into Newcastle – Coastline, Go Ahead Gateshead, Northern, VFM Buses and Wear Buses. Go Ahead Northern progressed further with the purchase of Low Fell Coaches in June 1992 and by 1994 had renamed itself the Go Ahead Group as it expanded in other parts of the country and prepared for a stock market flotation in May 1994. Newcastle's two other major operators changed ownership in 1994. In July Busways was acquired by Stagecoach Holdings and at about the same time Northumbria was sold to British Bus Group. Then in March 1995 the 225 vehicle OK Travel business was sold to the Go Ahead Group.

In many ways the activity over the last ten years on the ownership front has produced just as much change as the deregulation of bus services. Indeed the fact that Newcastle has never had a single dominant bus operator has probably had a major influence on events since 1986. Certainly the competitive initiatives of new operators, both medium sized and small, led to new facilities for passengers but the ongoing presence of several large operators has most likely more than any other factor ensured that bus services have continued to develop to meet the needs of the city.

I hope that readers of this book will enjoy the illustrations and their captions and gain interest from the wide variety of buses which have served Newcastle over the last 40 years. This book has not been produced to give detailed historical information about the operators. However, a summary of historical information for the larger operators is given overleaf and information for the smaller operators is set out in appropriate captions.

Finally, I would like to acknowledge the assistance of good friends who have supplied illustrations for this book. David Little, who has faithfully recorded the bus scene over many years, provided much of the material I required and appropriate illustrations from earlier years were kindly supplied by Robert C. Davis and Arnold Richardson/Photobus.

G. E. Hutchinson FCIT
May 1996

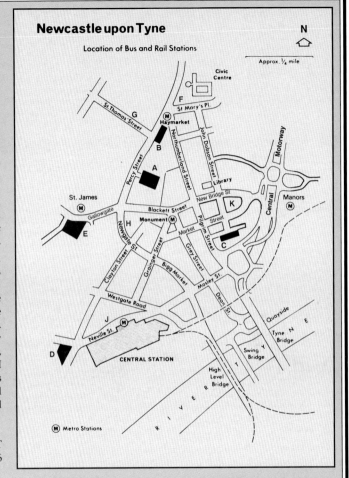

Newcastle upon Tyne

Location of Bus and Rail Stations

N

Approx. ¼ mile

Ⓜ Metro Stations

Bus Stations		**Street Bus Stands**	
A	Eldon Square	F	St. Mary's Place
B	Haymarket	G	St. Thomas' Street
C	Worswick Street (closed)	H	Newgate Street
D	Marlborough Crescent (closed)	J	Central Station area
E	Gallowgate (Coach Station)	K	Croft Street (closed)

HISTORICAL INFORMATION

NEWCASTLE CORPORATION
TYNESIDE/TYNE AND WEAR PASSENGER
  TRANSPORT EXECUTIVE
BUSWAYS TRAVEL SERVICES LTD

Local public transport in Newcastle commenced in 1878 when Newcastle Corporation constructed a system of horse tramways which was leased to a private company, the Newcastle and Gosforth Tramways and Carriage Co Ltd. In 1899 the Corporation obtained powers to electrify the system and it introduced electric trams in 1901 which it operated itself. The tramway system reached its peak in 1928 and the final trams were withdrawn in 1950. The trolleybus system was introduced on 1st October 1935 and the network became one of the largest in the United Kingdom. Withdrawal commenced in 1963 and was completed on 1st October 1966. Motor bus services were introduced by the Corporation in 1912 and expansion was rapid after the First World War. The network was known as Blue Bus Services until the yellow livery was adopted in 1949. The Corporation's bus services were transferred to the Tyneside Passenger Transport Executive on 1st January 1970. This became the Tyne and Wear Passenger Transport Executive from 1st April 1974. On 26th October 1986 the Executive's bus operations were transferred to Busways Travel Services Ltd, initially owned by the Tyne and Wear Passenger Transport Authority. On 5th May 1989 Busways was purchased by its senior management and employees who sold the company to Stagecoach Holdings on 26th July 1994.

THE NORTHERN GENERAL TRANSPORT CO LTD
  AND ASSOCIATED COMPANIES
GO AHEAD NORTHERN LTD
GO AHEAD GROUP PLC

The Northern General Transport Co Ltd commenced operations on 1st January 1914 and had been formed to consolidate the bus interests of the British Electric Traction Company's electric tramway undertakings in the area. These were Gateshead and District, Tynemouth and District and Jarrow and District which had commenced services in 1883 (Gateshead and Tynemouth) and 1906 (Jarrow). The initial services at Gateshead were steam hauled whilst those at Tynemouth were horse drawn. Electrification of both took place in 1901. Northern General expanded rapidly and became associated with the London and North Eastern Railway Company in 1929. Major acquisitions by Northern General included Sunderland District (1931) Tyneside Tramways (1936) and Venture Transport (1970). Northern General and its associated companies was one of the British Electric Traction Company's major bus and coach operating businesses and its fleet size peaked at 982 vehicles in 1954. Northern General became part of the National Bus Company from 1st January 1969. It was purchased on 7th May 1987 by Go Ahead Northern Ltd which was a new company formed for the purpose by its senior management team. This was renamed the Go Ahead Group Ltd and a stock market flotation followed in May 1994.

UNITED AUTOMOBILE SERVICES LTD
NORTHUMBRIA MOTOR SERVICES LTD

United was founded in April 1912 by E. B. Hutchinson with its head office at Lowestoft. Its initial operations were in East Anglia but after the First World War expansion took place in Derbyshire, Lincolnshire and the North East. In 1929 the company was acquired by Tilling and British Automobile Traction Ltd and the London and North Eastern Railway Company Ltd. In 1930/31 reorganisation enabled United to concentrate on its North East business. Many acquisitions were undertaken and the company operated a vast network of bus services in an area from Berwick to Bridlington and reaching westwards to Carlisle. In 1942 United became a subsidiary of Tilling Motor Services Ltd but still with the LNER shareholding and nationalisation followed in 1948. The United fleet contained over 1,000 vehicles in the mid to late 1950s. United became part of the National Bus Company from 1st January 1969. On 7th September 1986, prior to privatisation and deregulation, it was split into three parts with its northern division becoming Northumbria Motor Services Ltd. Northumbria was purchased by its senior management team on 21st October 1987 who sold the company to the British Bus Group in July 1994.

THE VENTURE TRANSPORT CO (NEWCASTLE) LTD

Venture Transport was formed in 1938 as an amalgamation of the businesses of Reed Brothers, Venture Bus Services and Robson Brothers (Yellow Bus Services). These concerns had been pioneer bus operators in the Derwent Valley area of north west County Durham with Reed Brothers having commenced running between Sunniside and Bensham tram terminus in 1912. The Venture business was progressively developed and by the early 1960s operated a modern fleet of 95 vehicles. It was sold to Northern General on 30th April 1970.

O.K. MOTOR SERVICES LTD
E. HOWE (O.K. MOTOR SERVICES) LTD

Wade Emmerson commenced operations in the Bishop Auckland area in 1912 and this business was, in 1959, formed into the limited company O.K. Motor Services Ltd. In 1928 E. Howe and W. Emmerson jointly commenced their service between Bishop Auckland and Newcastle. O.K. Motor Services Ltd expanded steadily and had a fleet of 41 vehicles when it acquired E. Howe's 6-vehicle business in 1968. Major expansion took place between 1986 and 1995 when the 225 vehicle business was acquired by the Go Ahead Group.

PART ONE

1956 - 1969

Services began on Newcastle Corporation's trolleybus system on 1st October 1935 and it became one of the largest in Great Britain. The system had a 31-year life and during that time nearly 350 trolleybuses ran on the network of services. The city boundary at Denton Square was the most westerly point on the system.

This 1965 picture at Denton Square turning circle shows fleet No. 596 (NBB 596) one of the final 1950 batch of 50 BUT 9641T MCCW 70-seat bodied vehicles.

The final services on the Newcastle trolleybus system were withdrawn on 1st October 1966 – exactly 31 years to the day since commencement. The process

of closure had started on 2nd June 1993 with Leyland Atlanteans taking over on service 34 between Denton Square and Wallsend via City Road and Walker Road. The last routes on the system were services 35, 35A and 35C between Denton Square, Brighton Grove, Delaval Road and Walker via Blackett Street and

Welbeck Road. The Newcastle trolleybus system was a substantial operation and the level of services can perhaps be best explained by quoting the frequency of vehicles in Grainger Street, the busiest part of the system. In January 1962 there were 84 scheduled trolleybuses per hour in each direction.

Right:

Newcastle Corporation motor bus services commenced in 1912 and were initially developed as tramway feeders. However, services were soon introduced to towns and villages outside the city. By the 1920s the bus routes were known as 'Blue Bus Services' because of the blue livery used on the vehicles. One of the earliest routes was that to Ponteland village which commenced in 1921. After the Second World War double-deck vehicles were used on some journeys to Ponteland but, until it was raised in 1969, a low bridge at Kenton Bank Foot caused low-height vehicles to be necessary. This mid-1960s view shows fleet No. 354 (LVK 6) leaving Haymarket bus station for Ponteland and the nearby Darras Hall Estate. This low-height Leyland-bodied Leyland PD2 was one of six delivered in 1949

and was one of the last vehicles delivered in blue livery, though it is shown here in yellow of course. This bus continued to be used on service 5 to Ponteland until 1969 when it was transferred to driver training duties.

Facing page, lower left:

The six low-height Leyland double-deckers were supplemented by ten more low-height vehicles in 1957 which in the main replaced a batch of ten Daimler CVD6 single-deckers which were also used on the Ponteland service. The ten new low-height double-deckers were 58-seat Park Royal-bodied AEC Regent V models. Fleet No.158 (158 AVK) was photographed in August 1968 leaving Haymarket bus station for Ponteland and Darras Hall. This bus was withdrawn in 1969.

Facing page upper right:

This picture, taken at Throckley terminus in 1966, shows fleet No. 274 (NBB 274) a 1949 AEC Regent III with Northern Coachbuilders bodywork. This was one of the first batch of motor buses delivered in what was essentially the yellow trolleybus livery and which thereafter replaced the blue motor bus livery. The lengthy bus route from the Central Station to Lemington, Newburn and Throckley had replaced the tramway service in 1946. By 1953 it was extended via the Tyne Bridge to Heworth and later to the Leam Lane and Wardley areas of Gateshead and Felling. It then became one of the joint services with Gateshead and District although all regular workings were undertaken by Newcastle Corporation vehicles. Fleet No. 274 was withdrawn soon after this picture was taken.

Facing page lower right:

The first 8ft-wide buses for Newcastle Corporation were delivered in 1950. One of these was fleet No. 308 (NVK 308) a Leyland PD2 with 56-seat Leyland bodywork. This 1965 picture was taken at Fawdon Park Road terminus. Service 7 between Fawdon and Springwell via the Tyne Bridge was one of the many cross-Tyne services operated jointly with Gateshead and District. Fleet No. 308 had given nineteen years' service to its owners by the time of its withdrawal in 1969.

Above: In 1956 Newcastle Corporation took delivery of twenty 62-seat AEC Regent V double-deckers with Park Royal bodywork. This 1965 photograph shows fleet No. 152 (XVK 152) at Barras Bridge near Haymarket operating west bound on service 2. This route was successor to one of the earliest motor bus routes wholly within the city which had been introduced in the 1920s to cover areas not served by tramway services. This rather circuitous route avoided direct competition with the tramway services but over the years it was developed into one of the city's busiest cross-city routes. Fleet No. 152 was transferred to Tyneside PTE on 1st January 1970.

By the end of the 1960s Newcastle Corporation's early post-war fleet was being replaced by deliveries of new Leyland Atlanteans. However, this April 1968 picture, taken at Morden Street bus park near Haymarket, shows two elderly vehicles resting after operating peak hour duplicates. Fleet No. 420 (LVK 120) was a 1948 Leyland-bodied Leyland PD2. It makes an interesting comparison with fleet No. 321 (NVK 321) a 1950 AEC Regent III with Northern Coachbuilders bodywork. Both vehicles were withdrawn from service in 1969.

Newcastle Corporation was an early convert to the Leyland Atlantean with the first examples arriving in 1960 and regular deliveries thereafter. Fleet No. 245 (KBB 245D) was an Alexander-bodied example delivered in 1966. It was photographed in March 1968 in Neville Street, opposite Newcastle Central Station, awaiting departure for Heaton Road and Jesmond Road on service 42. This route had replaced a similar trolleybus route at the end of May 1965. The Atlantean in the background is an earlier Weymann-bodied example.

Following the withdrawals of trams, a process which was concluded in 1951, the replacement Gateshead and District motor buses were painted in a maroon and cream livery. The original tramway replacement buses were Guy Arab and Leyland PD2 double-deckers but from 1959 onwards the Leyland Atlantean became the dominant vehicle type in the fleet. In a similar manner to the tram services, most of the replacement bus services were operated jointly with Newcastle Corporation as cross-river services via either the Tyne Bridge or High Level Bridge. This early 1960s picture taken at the depot shows Gateshead and District No. 65 (CCN 165) a 1951 Leyland-bodied Leyland PD2.

From 1964 the Gateshead and District fleet livery was changed to green and cream similar to that used by fellow Northern General subsidiary Tyneside. This mid-1960s picture taken near Haymarket shows Gateshead and District fleet No. 80 (KCN 180). This Alexander-bodied vehicle was the first of the initial batch of Atlanteans delivered in 1959. It was photographed whilst operating south-bound on joint service 28 to Low Fell and Calderwood Crescent. Also visible in this picture are a United Bristol Lodekka, a Newcastle Corporation Leyland PD2 and an unidentified Weymann Fanfare-bodied coach.

The Tyneside Tramways and Tramroads Company was the smallest Northern General subsidiary concentrating mainly on stage-carriage operations. Tyneside was acquired by Northern General in 1936 and its main activity was the frequent service between Croft Street, Wallsend and North Shields which was operated jointly with Newcastle Corporation between Croft Street and Wallsend. This early 1960s view shows Tyneside fleet No. 41 (GTY 171) a 1954 Metro Cammell-bodied Leyland PD2 passing the Trafalgar en route for Croft Street.

In 1965 the Tyneside company was renamed The Tyneside Omnibus Company Limited and from 1964 onwards it received regular small intakes of Leyland Atlanteans for its fleet. This picture shows fleet No. 57 (HJR 657D) one of two Alexander-bodied Atlanteans delivered in 1966. It was photographed whilst still new operating towards Newcastle on the main service from North Shields and Wallsend.

The Tynemouth and District fleet received many Guy Arab double-deckers in the years after the Second World War with regular deliveries until 1956. These vehicles were frequently employed on services 5 and 11 between Haymarket and Whitley Bay or Tynemouth via the Coast Road. This picture, taken in 1964, shows fleet No. 188 (FT 7388), a 1952 Weymann-bodied Guy Arab III, which was on this occasion operating North Shields local service number 15.

Wakefield's Motors Limited had been placed under the control of Tynemouth and District in 1932 after its acquisition by Northern General in 1929. Wakefield's buses could be seen in Newcastle on the service to Tynemouth via the Coast Road operated jointly with Tynemouth and District and Newcastle Corporation. From 1st January 1970 the activities of Wakefield's Motors were absorbed by Tynemouth and District. This photograph shows Wakefield's fleet No. 304 (EFT 704F) an Alexander-bodied Leyland Leopard one of two which joined the fleet in 1968.

The Sunderland District Omnibus Company of Philadelphia, County Durham had been a Northern General subsidiary since 1931 and its vehicles could be seen in Newcastle at Worswick Street bus station. Ten Leyland Royal Tigers with Brush 43-seat bodywork joined the fleet in 1951 and could often be seen at Worswick Street during the 1950s. This particular photograph of fleet No. 240 (LUP 391) was taken at Consett in the early 1960s with the bus awaiting departure on the 90-minute journey to Sunderland on service 15 which was a joint operation with Northern General.

In 1947 Northern General took delivery of eighteen Brush-bodied AEC Regals which could often be seen on services into Newcastle during the 1950s. This photograph, taken at Stanley depot, shows fleet number 1144 (CN 9984). These buses had a seating capacity of 36.

The Northern General fleet included a large number of single and double-deck Guy Arab vehicles. The penultimate batch of double-deckers of this make was delivered in 1955, fitted with Weymann bodies. Fleet No. 1643 (CU 7643) was photographed at Hartlepool in the early 1960s prior to departing on the two hour journey to Newcastle on service 45 via Peterlee, Houghton-le-Spring and Chester-le-Street. This service was operated jointly with United Automobile Services.

In 1954 Northern General received fifteen SARO-bodied Leyland Tiger Cubs and a further sixteen were delivered to associated company Sunderland District. In 1961 three of the Sunderland District vehicles were transferred to Northern General. Fleet No. 1994 (OUP 655) was photographed in 1965 travelling south-bound from the Tyne Bridge on service 82. This was a complex local service which linked parts of inner Gateshead and Felling to Newcastle Central Station. It was unusual at the time in that all of Northern's services except this one terminated at one of the city's bus stations.

In 1955 Northern General took delivery of 22 underfloor-engined Guy Arab single-deckers with Weymann bodywork. This picture was taken at Winlaton depot in 1964 and shows fleet No. 1672 (SPT 72). The bus had arrived from Newcastle's Marlborough Crescent bus station on the half-hourly service 8. The destination shown is Winlaton Flight. This indicated the terminus near to Winlaton Aerial Flight which was an overhead conveyor system for carrying locally-mined coal. Northern's services in the Winlaton area had been obtained in 1951 with the acquisition of the twelve-vehicle business of J. W. Hurst & Sons Ltd.

By the end of the 1960s Northern General was giving attention to innovative new designs for its fleet. A unique delivery in 1967 was fleet No. 2332 (ECN 32E) a Leyland Leopard with the prototype Marshall Camair body. This picture was taken at Marlborough Crescent bus station on 8th April 1968 and the bus is awaiting departure for Winlaton via Swalwell on service 117. One of the subsequent order for Marshall Camair bodies for the Northern Group is shown on page 36.

Left:

The Bristol L type single-decker bus with standard ECW bodywork was an important type of vehicle in the fleet of United Automobile Services until the final ones were withdrawn in 1966. These buses could be seen in Newcastle on a wide variety of United services. Fleet No. G416 (LHN 863) was a 1950 Bristol L5G which was photographed in 1965 at Alnwick. By this stage it had been converted for 'pay as you enter' operation. It was resting between duties on service 77 between Alnwick and Boulmer on to which connections could be made at Alnwick from service 12 from Newcastle. Service 12 operated basically hourly between Newcastle, Morpeth, Alnwick, Berwick and Edinburgh jointly with Scottish Omnibuses (SMT).

Below left:

United operated a substantial fleet of Bristol K-type double-deckers with both low-height and normal-height ECW bodywork. Fleet No. 74 (WHN 56) was a 1954 normal-height KSW6B and was photographed in 1970 at Jesmond Road depot, Newcastle.

Opposite page top left:

On 5th January 1969, five days into the National Bus Company era, the Carlisle depot of United and 21 vehicles were transferred to Ribble Motor Services. Thus Ribble became joint operator of service 334 between Newcastle and Carlisle. Shortly after the transfer former United fleet No. U189 (689 BHN) was photographed in the erstwhile United bus station at Carlisle having arrived from Newcastle. This 1956 ECW-bodied Bristol LS5G had become Ribble fleet No. 261 but was still painted in full United livery. This was the oldest vehicle transferred. It had also been intended to transfer three Bristol KSW6B vehicles but Ribble reinstated three Leyland PD2 buses instead.

Above right:

United Automobile Services had a substantial fleet of ECW-bodied Bristol MW5G single-deckers. Fleet No. U555 (555 LHN) was built in 1959 and was photographed at one of the bus stands in St. Thomas' Street in early 1968. Service 17 between Newcastle and Whitley Bay via Clousden Hill, West Allotment and Earsdon was an important service which operated every fifteen minutes daily.

Right:

United fleet No. RS13 (PHN 613F) was a 1967 ECW-bodied Bristol RESL6G. This was one of a batch of twenty buses that were the company's first short length Bristol RE saloons. It was photographed in St. Thomas' Street in 1968 awaiting departure on the Dudley circular service 350. The complex half-hourly services 350/351 which operated north of the city into north Tyneside, had a round trip scheduled journey time of 82 minutes requiring an allocation of three buses.

Left:

Venture Transport of Consett, County Durham was the largest independent company providing services into Newcastle. Major fleet renewal had taken place between 1946 and 1948 with the acquisition of 60 Daimler CVD6 saloons with 35-seat Willowbrook bodies. Indeed no more new vehicles were delivered until 24 Willowbrook-bodied underfloor-engined Atkinson Alpha saloons arrived between 1955 and 1957. This photograph was taken in the early 1960s and shows fleet No. 164 (JPT 552), the penultimate Daimler CVD6, which was new in 1948 and remained in service until 1964 by which time it had been converted for 'pay as you enter' operation. The bus was parked at Marlborough Crescent bus station prior to departure on service 44 to Rockwood Hill via Folly.

Lower left:

Venture Transport turned to the Albion Aberdonian for its new vehicle deliveries in 1958 and 1959. Seventeen of these were purchased all with Willowbrook bodywork. Fleet No. 203 (167 BUP) was photographed in 1964 at North Wylam proceeding to Rockwood Gardens, Greenside. On arrival at Rockwood Gardens (sometimes known as Rockwood Hill) the bus would take up service 44 to Newcastle's Marlborough Crescent bus station. The final batch of six Albion Aberdonians (201-206) weighed only 4 tons 19cwt unladen. They were very economical although their drivers had to handle the constant mesh gearbox with skill in Venture's hilly territory.

Facing page, lower:

For 40 years the OK route between Bishop Auckland and Newcastle was in fact operated by two concerns – OK Motor Services Ltd, owned by the Emmerson family and E. Howe (OK Motor Services) Ltd. The Howe business was acquired by OK Motor Services Ltd in 1968. This photograph was taken at the end of the 1960s and shows the 1958 Roe-bodied Leyland PD3 of OK Motor Services Ltd (YUP 487) which was a regular performer on the Newcastle service for many years. It had just passed the Central Station and was approaching Marlborough Crescent bus station.

Upper left:

OK Motor Services Ltd purchased its first 36ft-long single-decker in 1962. This 55-seat Plaxton-bodied AEC Reliance (399 UP) soon became a familiar sight on the Newcastle service. In this illustration it is seen leaving Marlborough Crescent bus station for Bishop Auckland in the mid-1960s.

Upper right:

The fleet of E. Howe (OK Motor Services) Ltd was always all single-deck and the main activity was participation in the Bishop Auckland-Newcastle service. This picture was taken in the early 1960s and shows Howe's 1956 Roe-bodied AEC Reliance (RUP 508) leaving the Gateshead end of the High Level bridge en route for Bishop Auckland.

NW Norfolk commenced business in 1926. He gained a licence in 1931 to operate from Kilnpit Hill to Newcastle. By the 1960s the business was still operating several journeys a day into Marlborough Crescent bus station from Scales Cross, Apperley Dene and Stocksfield via Crawcrook and Ryton. However, a licence condition imposing protective fares on the busiest section of the route between Stocksfield and Newcastle (where United and Venture were the main operators) meant that the service was always at a disadvantage. Despite this the small business carried on and some reduction in the protective conditions had been granted in 1957. However, United took over the service from 1st July 1964. This picture was taken shortly before then and shows two of Norfolk's Duple-bodied Dennis Lancets at Marlborough Crescent bus station (CNL 413 and DNL 832).

Mr W. M. Appleby of Choppington, Northumberland had since 1938 operated between Morpeth and Newcastle via Ponteland. In addition for a period between 1962 and 1966 he operated the Newcastle, Ponteland, Otterburn service. Appleby used the fleet name Terrier Coaches for many years. This 1966 photograph shows his Beadle-bodied Commer TS3 (CSY 38) awaiting departure from Morpeth for Ponteland and Newcastle.

R. Armstrong (Bus Proprietor) Ltd originated as a miners' contract operator in 1930 later developing its private hire work. In August 1954 Armstrong took over the Newcastle, Stamfordham, Matfen service from Bell's Services Ltd which was a subsidiary of United Automobile Services. This daily rural service provided ten journeys on weekdays, thirteen on Saturdays and five on Sundays with some weekend journeys extended to Ryal, Ingoe, Walridge or Kirkheaton. By the mid-1960s Venture Transport was starting to dispose of its Atkinson single-deckers and a number were sold to smaller independent operators in Northumberland. Armstrong bought two in 1966. This picture shows former Venture Transport fleet No. 166 (RPT 126) at Stamfordham in 1967 awaiting departure for Newcastle, Newgate Street via Westerhope.

The T. B. Vasey business originally commenced in 1955 to take over the Newcastle, Ponteland, Otterburn service from Galleys Motors of Newcastle. At a later stage, in 1960, Galleys was acquired by R. Armstrong (Bus Proprietor) Ltd. T. B. Vasey actually ceased operating the Otterburn service in 1962, when Terrier Coaches took over, but in 1966 re-acquired the service. This 1966 photograph shows T. B. Vasey's Yeates-bodied Bedford SB (XYG1) at the Bay Horse Inn, West Woodburn on what was at that time a Saturdays only extension to Ridsdale of the Newcastle-Otterburn service. Another operator, Rochester and Marshall of Great Whittington, served West Woodburn from Newcastle via Stamfordham on Fridays, Saturdays and Sundays. This had been taken over from Galleys Motors in 1955 but was withdrawn in 1964.

M. Charlton and Sons of Newbrough near Hexham had operated into Hexham from after the First World War and the business expanded after the Second World War with workers' contract services. In 1958 the old-established business of Cecil Moffit of Acomb, near Hexham was acquired including a daily service between Bellingham, Heddon and Newcastle. In 1961 Charlton's business was acquired by Mid Tyne Transport Ltd which continued to trade as M. Charlton. Mid Tyne Transport was acquired by Tyne Valley Coaches Ltd in 1967. The Newcastle-Bellingham service was eventually withdrawn by Tyne Valley in 1971. This early 1960s picture shows Mid Tyne Transport No. 45 (STY 429) a Bedford SB1 with Duple Midland 43-seat bodywork at Haymarket bus station awaiting departure for Bellingham.

PART TWO
1970-1986

Tyneside PTE No. 472 (175 AVK) was a 1957 AEC Regent V with 62-seat Park Royal bodywork which originated with Newcastle Corporation Transport. It had originally been fleet No. 175 and was renumbered shortly after transfer to the PTE. It is seen in Dean Street on 13th February 1971 operating service 15, the Jesmond Circle. This service was in fact withdrawn on 21st March 1971 causing the last former Newcastle Corporation half-cab buses to be withdrawn. Dean Street is typical of the steep gradients experienced in some parts of Newcastle.

Tyneside PTE No. 514 (UVK 514G) was a 1969 Leyland Panther with 45-seat Alexander bodywork. This illustration at Newcastle Central Station on 12th June 1971 shows service 42, the Spital Tongues/ Heaton Road Circle which had been introduced on 21st March 1971 by linking together two previously separate circular services. All fourteen Leyland Panthers in the Newcastle fleet were transferred to the PTE's South Shields depot in exchange for eleven Bristol RESL saloons in 1974.

Newcastle Corporation was an early convert to the Leyland Atlantean with large fleet intakes from 1960 onwards. This view of Tyneside PTE No. 202 (202 JVK) a 1961 example with Weymann 78-seat bodywork shows the initial Tyneside PTE livery as adopted from Newcastle Corporation with the addition of the PTE symbol. The bus is seen on 1st July 1972 at Haymarket on service 67 to Leam Lane Estate, Gateshead, a joint service with Gateshead and District.

Tyneside PTE No. 601 (KBB 251D) was a 1966 Leyland Atlantean with Alexander 78-seat bodywork which was converted to two-door 70-seat layout by Newcastle Corporation in 1968. It had previously been fleet No. 251 and was the prototype for a batch of fifteen Atlanteans with forward ascending nearside staircases delivered in 1968 and 1969. The nearside staircase two-door double-decker was to remain unique to Newcastle and the PTE with the last new vehicles with this layout being delivered in 1978. Number 601 is seen at New Bridge Street on 19th August 1972 amidst Central Motorway construction on busy cross-city service 37.

Tyneside PTE No. 395 (ACU 25C) was a South Shields depot former South Shields Corporation 76-seat Roe-bodied Daimler Fleetline. It was photographed on 25th November 1973 at Central Station on service 33 west-bound to Fenham via Elswick Road. The bus was on temporary reallocation to Slatyford Lane depot at the time of a trial of Autofare ticketing equipment which was not adopted by the PTE. However, the main purpose of the reallocation was to evaluate the Fleetline in Newcastle compared with the Atlantean. In the event the PTE kept its Fleetlines south of the Tyne at its South Shields and Sunderland depots.

Tyneside PTE became the Tyne and Wear PTE from 1st April 1974. Fleet No. 341 (ECU 201E) was photographed at Bewick Street, Central Station on service 41 on 3rd April 1974. The PTE inherited eleven Bristol RESL saloons from South Shields Corporation and these were transferred to Newcastle in 1974 in exchange for Leyland Panthers. When the Bristol RE became available on the open market South Shields Corporation had been an early customer for this model for its first one-person-operated services in 1967. Number 341 was originally fleet No. 1 in the South Shields fleet and is now preserved in the Corporation's blue livery.

Tyne and Wear PTE No. 401 (GCN 1N) was an Alexander-bodied Ailsa, one of a batch of three, delivered in 1975. It is seen entering Market Street on 25th February 1976 having passed under new hotel construction travelling west on busy cross-city service 12 to Two Ball Lonnen. The bus is in the happily short-lived simplified version of the initial PTE livery which omitted the traditional Newcastle yellow colour from between the decks and was not well received at the time. The three Ailsa vehicles were withdrawn and sold in 1978.

Tyne and Wear PTE No. 709 (GBB 509K) was a 1972 10 metre-length Alexander-bodied 78-seat Leyland Atlantean with two doors and a nearside staircase. It was one of a batch of 25 vehicles and is shown in the new yellow and white livery which was introduced to brighten fleet appearance. Number 709 was photographed in Grainger Street on 22nd September 1976 on the long cross-city service 20 between Wallsend and Throckley.

In 1977 (for The Queen's Silver Jubilee) and 1978 (for the Centenary of local public transport in Tyne and Wear) the PTE provided a special service using a preserved Leyland PD2 and a preserved AEC Regent III. The Leyland PD2 was painted in the Newcastle blue livery which was used on motor buses until 1949. This picture shows the Leyland PD2, fleet No. 123 (LVK 123), arriving at Central Station from Gosforth Park on 1st June 1977. This particular bus had in fact been delivered new in this livery in 1948 although it would have gained the yellow livery a few years later. It was finally withdrawn from regular service in 1969.

Tyne and Wear PTE No. 422 (OTN 422R) is seen arriving at Central Station on 15th July 1977. It was one of 140 MCW Metropolitans placed in service by the PTE between 1975 and 1977 all of which were based at the two Newcastle depots. These smooth and lively buses were popular with passengers and crews but nearly all were withdrawn by 1986 as body corrosion problems took their toll. Service 62 from Killingworth New Town to the city centre was a component part of a busy group of services providing a five-minute headway between Benton Four Lane Ends and the city via Chillingham Road.

Whilst the Tyne and Wear Metro was under construction the PTE operated special 'Rail Link' bus services to cover the period between the withdrawal of the British Rail diesel rail car services and the introduction of Metro services. The 'Rail Link' services were operated from various PTE, Northern and United depots using a dedicated fleet of PTE vehicles which over the years comprised of various batches of Leyland Atlanteans. There was one non-standard vehicle however, a Cardiff City Transport Bristol VRT which was on extended loan in exchange for a PTE coach required to expand the Cardiff coach fleet. This illustration at Sandyford Road, Jesmond on 19th July 1978 shows Tyne and Wear PTE No. 624 (SVK 624G) and Cardiff City Transport No. 600 (PKG 600M) both bound for West Monkseaton.

Snow conditions can cause problems, particularly in hilly areas like some parts of the west end of Newcastle. This particular illustration shows Tyne and Wear PTE No. 551 (MVK 551R) a 1976 Leyland Atlantean with nearside staircase Alexander body, along with another Atlantean, in difficulty on Atkinson Road on the long cross-city service 2 from Walker to Cowgate, Montagu Estate. This route does not now exist in this form. However, Atlantean No. 551 was still in operation at Blue Bus Services in 1996.

In another snow scene Tyne and Wear PTE No. 734 (LBB 734P) a 1976 MCW Metropolitan is seen picking up passengers at Sandyford Road, Jesmond westbound for Fenham on service 33.

The penultimate batch of Leyland Atlanteans for Tyne and Wear PTE was made up of fifty 10 metre chassis with 86-seat Alexander bodies. These fine vehicles served Newcastle well for over fifteen years on some of the heaviest cross-city routes such as service 21 between Wallsend and Throckley. This picture of fleet No. 135 (AVK 135V) was taken at Central Station on 27th August 1980 when the bus was still almost new. The bus in the background is one of the 1979 batch of 10 metre Atlanteans. The 50 vehicles in this batch were the last bodies produced by MCW for another manufacturer's chassis and these buses were all sold to Northern General in 1982/83.

Tyne and Wear PTE No. 413 (JFT 413X) was one of two Alexander-bodied Scania BR112 vehicles purchased in 1982 for evaluation. This picture was taken on 15th September 1982 at Central Station with the bus waiting to depart on the long outer circular route via the city's western and northern suburbs to Four Lane Ends Metro interchange. The destination blinds were designed to fit in with the promotion of the integrated bus and Metro system. The depot code (NS) for Newcastle Slatyford Lane depot is also visible by the front fleet number.

The old established Newcastle bus and coach business R. Armstrong (Bus Proprietor) Ltd and its associated company Galleys Coaches Ltd were purchased by Tyneside PTE on 24th August 1973 and formed the basis of the PTE's coaching division Armstrong Galley. Armstrongs operated a stage carriage service between Newgate Street and Stamfordham, Matfen and various villages about fifteen miles west of Newcastle and this Leyland RTL (KXW 19) was often used for peak hours duplication on the Westerhope-Newgate Street section of this route. The bus is seen on 31st March 1974 turning from Newgate Street into Grainger Street with the author at the wheel.

Mr W. M. Appleby's Terrier Coaches business was renamed as Highway International by the early 1970s and continued its three-times-daily service between Morpeth, Ponteland and Newcastle, Haymarket. This picture, taken at Morpeth bus station in 1973, shows Appleby's new Willowbrook-bodied Bedford YRT (HNL 346L) awaiting departure for Newcastle. Appleby abandoned this service on 13th September 1975 and a replacement facility was provided by Tyne and Wear PTE and then subsequently Blue Bus Services.

Gateshead and District No. 78 (HCN 478) was a 1958 Leyland PD3 with MCW 73-seat bodywork. This was one of a batch of five vehicles which were Gateshead's last new front-engined buses as the Leyland Atlantean became increasingly dominant in the fleet from 1960 onwards. The bus is seen in Northumberland Road on 29th June 1970 on the joint cross-river service with Tyneside PTE to Dunston via the High Level bridge.

Thirteen of Northern General's 1972 ECW-bodied Leyland Atlanteans were allocated from new to Gateshead and District. Fleet No. 103L (NCN 103L) is seen in Westgate Road having left Central Station on the Saltwell Park/Bensham circular service 54 on 17th August 1974. Services 53/54 were short high frequency cross-river routes licensed jointly with Tyne and Wear PTE but all regular scheduled workings were undertaken by Gateshead and District.

Gateshead and District operated sixteen Park Royal-bodied Leyland Atlanteans delivered in 1974 and displaying the newly adopted NBC version of the PTE's yellow livery. Fleet No. 210N (RCN 110N) was photographed in Grainger Street on 4th September 1974 operating north-bound on service 25 which was another joint cross-river service with Tyne and Wear PTE. At the end of December 1975 Gateshead and District ceased trading and was absorbed by Northern General.

Tyneside gained its first ever single-deckers in 1969. These were two Leyland Panthers with Marshall Camair bodies part of an order for 25 such vehicles for the Northern group. As well as the main service between Croft Street and North Shields, Tyneside buses were to be seen on an infrequent route between Wallsend and Gosforth and various special works services mainly provided for various riverside industries including the shipyards. Fleet No. 61 (RJR 61G) was photographed at Croft Street on 30th May 1970 awaiting departure on a works service to Howdon, Tyne Tunnel.

The Tyneside fleet was also converted to the yellow livery in the early 1970s. This photograph, taken at Croft Street in October 1975, shows 1968 Alexander-bodied Leyland Atlantean fleet No. 60 (NNL 60F). By this time the service to North Shields had been allocated a route number – 313. However, the end was near for Tyneside as it was absorbed by its parent Northern General at the end of December 1975. The PTE Atlantean in the background was fleet No. 424 (224 JVK) an Alexander-bodied vehicle dating from 1962. It was proceeding west-bound on service 39 to Denton Square.

Tyneside operated its main service between Croft Street, Wallsend and North Shields on a ten-minute frequency. This service was in fact jointly operated with the PTE between Croft Street and Wallsend with PTE buses providing a further six journeys per hour to produce a five-minute frequency. Tyneside No. 49 (NNL 49) was photographed on 13th March 1970 in New Bridge Street en route for North Shields. It was a 1958 Leyland PD3 with a 73-seat MCW body. This bus was rebuilt in 1972 to normal control configuration to enable one-person operation.

Northern General No. 3000 (MCN 30K) was built in 1972 from Tyneside No. 49 and given the name 'Tynesider'. Its normal control layout was an attempt at producing a front-engined bus suitable for one person operation. The project was not pursued and the bus saw little use after the end of 1972 until its withdrawal in 1978. This picture was taken on 19th August 1972. It was operating on the Tyneside North Shields service in New Bridge Street, Newcastle during the course of Central Motorway construction. A less radical conversion was undertaken on Routemaster No. 2085 by moving the cab backwards and siting it more adjacent to the entrance to produce a semi-normal control layout. This was given the name 'Wearsider' and it operated in this form from 1972 to 1978.

Left:

Tynemouth and District No. 224 (AFT 924) was a 1958 Leyland PD3 with MCW 73-seat bodywork. On 8th July 1971 it was photographed in Hartlepool bus station being operated by Northern General on service 40 to Sunderland and Newcastle. Hartlepool bus station was owned by United. The single-deck bus in the background is a Plaxton-bodied AEC Reliance of G. B. Motor Services which will have arrived from Durham or Bishop Auckland. This concern was acquired by United in 1974.

Below left:

Tynemouth and District standardised on the Daimler Fleetline for double-deckers from 1963 following three batches of Leyland Atlanteans. Fleet No. 270 (HFT 270) was a Weymann-bodied Fleetline from the first batch of ten vehicles delivered in 1963. It is seen at St. Mary's Place on 1st July 1972 awaiting departure for Whitley Bay on service 408 which was operated jointly with United.

Opposite page:

Tynemouth and District vehicles were painted into yellow livery from 1973 onwards including this former East Yorkshire Park Royal-bodied AEC Renown fleet No. 331 (GAT 818D). It was photographed in Northumberland Road on 17th August 1974 proceeding towards St. Mary's Place for departure to Tynemouth on this joint service with Tyne and Wear PTE. At the end of 1974 Tynemouth and District was absorbed by Northern General.

Sunderland District No. 288 (YPT 288) was a 1958 Burlingham-bodied Leyland PD3. This picture was taken at Sunderland Park Lane bus station in 1970 and the bus is waiting to depart for Newcastle, Worswick Street on service 40 having just arrived from Hartlepool. This lengthy service was operated jointly with Northern General and United. This traditional version of the Sunderland District livery with larger areas of white relief was soon to be replaced by a simpler version with less white relief.

Sunderland District No. 312 (312 GPT) was a 1960 MCW-bodied 43-seat Leyland Tiger Cub. It is seen leaving Worswick Street bus station on 23rd August 1972 on service 39 bound for Houghton-le-Spring. Service 39 was a frequent, busy service from Newcastle to various industrial and mining areas in mid and east Durham operated jointly with Northern General and because of low bridges, restricted to single-deck operation. After the introduction of Metro service this route was truncated at Heworth interchange. Sunderland District's activities were absorbed by Northern General at the end of 1974.

Northern General 1827 (YPT 827) was a 1958 MCW-bodied Leyland PD3. It was photographed near Worswick Street bus station on 4th July 1970 prior to departing on service 24 to South Shields via Hebburn and Jarrow. At this time, on weekdays, Northern operated nine buses per hour between Newcastle and South Shields with extras at peak hours and on Saturdays. However, these all ceased to exist after the introduction of Metro service to South Shields in 1984.

This picture was taken at Worswick Street bus station on 16th January 1971 and shows two Northern General vehicles – 1965 Routemaster No. 2128 (FPT 598C) and 1960 MCW-bodied Leyland Atlantean No. 1899 (899 EUP). The Routemaster is awaiting departure on service 25 for Brady Square, Washington where increased traffic was being experienced as Washington new town developed. The Atlantean displays an experimental livery, which was not adopted, as it prepares for departure to South Shields on service 16.

In 1971 Northern General group received 33 Bristol RELL saloons. Fleet No. 2741 (KCN 241J) is seen when new on 22nd May 1971 entering Worswick Street bus station on service 120 from Lumley and Chester-le-Street. This Saturday-only facility was withdrawn in October 1971.

Northern General No. 1611 (DCN 911) was a 1954 AEC Park Royal Monocoach integral saloon which was photographed on 15th August 1971 having just left Marlborough Crescent bus station bound for Consett via Number One on service 33. This long-established half-hourly service followed hilly terrain over its fifteen-mile route from Tyneside to the steel-making town of Consett which is nearly 1,000ft above sea level. Number One appeared on the destination blinds of both Northern and Venture buses and is a small suburb of Consett named after number one mining shaft of many years earlier.

The first Leyland Nationals for Northern General joined the fleet in 1972 and were presented in the company's pre NBC livery. Fleet No. 5K (UUP 825K) was photographed on 20th August 1972 having just departed from Marlborough Crescent bus station on service 66, the Dunston circular. This short route operated four journeys per hour to the Dunston area of Gateshead with a round trip time of 25 minutes.

By 1973 Northern General's growing fleet of Leyland Nationals were appearing in standard NBC red livery. Fleet No. 145M (OCN 745M) is pictured on 3rd October 1973 leaving Marlborough Crescent bus station on service 2 bound for Quaking Houses. This was a mining village near Stanley, County Durham. Service 2 was one of a number of long-established routes from the city to the Stanley area of north-west County Durham, all of which were operated by Northern General.

Northern General introduced a new fleet numbering scheme in 1974 probably to take account of the impending absorption of the fleets of its various subsidiaries. Leyland National 5K was renumbered 4406 and this picture, taken on 29th March 1981, shows the bus in NBC style yellow livery and makes an interesting comparison with the illustration on the previous page. The bus was parked at Marlborough Crescent bus station having arrived on the lengthy and circuitous service 529 from South Shields.

This picture, with the roof of Marlborough Crescent bus station just visible, shows Northern General Leyland Leopard with Marshall bodywork No. 4089 (ECN 22E) on 10th May 1976. It is travelling empty having just arrived from Kibblesworth on service 91. It is overtaking a Southend Transport Daimler Fleetline operating on Tyne and Wear PTE service 2 which was one of a number of hired vehicles in use to overcome a vehicle shortage. In the distance is an O.K. Motor Services Plaxton-bodied Leyland Leopard arriving at Marlborough Crescent from Bishop Auckland.

In 1982/83 Northern General purchased 50 MCW-bodied Leyland Atlanteans from Tyne and Wear PTE. The bodies on these 86-seat 10 metre-long vehicles were the last produced by MCW for another manufacturer's chassis. Fleet No. 3707 (YNL 207V), dating from 1979, was photographed on 31st October 1982 passing Newcastle Central Station heading for Marlborough Crescent bus station on service 651 from Sunniside. The bus carries full Tyne and Wear livery as worn at this stage by NBC subsidiaries' vehicles operating on services within Tyne and Wear.

Northern General No. 3620 (A620 BCN) was a 1984 MCW Metrobus delivered in full Tyne and Wear livery. It was photographed on 30th May 1984 in Newgate Street having just left Eldon Square bus station on service X94 bound for Easington Lane. This hourly service operated on a limited-stop basis via Washington new town and Houghton-le-Spring to Easington Lane at the southern extremity of Tyne and Wear County. It was a good example of one of the through bus services to Newcastle from areas where more local services had been truncated at Heworth Metro interchange.

Northern General No. 3647 (A647 BCN) was a 1984 MCW Metrobus delivered in standard NBC red livery. On 26th August 1984 it was to be seen departing Worswick Street bus station for Durham on service 723. At this stage Worswick Street was much quieter than it had been in earlier years as a result of bus service changes resulting from the introduction of Metro services. However, the position was soon to change following bus service deregulation in 1986. Thereafter activity increased and levels of usage changed considerably until the bus station was finally closed on 1st April 1996.

United No. 4166 (LHN 266D) was a 1966 Bristol RELL which had been given a new ECW body in 1970 following an accident. This photograph, taken in September 1970 at Marlborough Crescent bus station, shows the bus preparing to pull on to its departure platform for Carlisle via Hexham. Service 334 was by this stage jointly operated with Ribble's Carlisle depot. The journey between Newcastle and Carlisle was scheduled to take three hours in 1970.

Ribble No. 892 (ECK 892E) was also photographed at Marlborough Crescent bus station in 1970 awaiting departure for Carlisle on service 334. This was one of fourteen Marshall-bodied Leyland Leopards delivered to Ribble in 1967 and provides an interesting comparison with the Bristol RELL illustrated above.

United Automobile Services was still organised and operated via four areas or divisions at the beginning of the 1970s. Most United buses running into Newcastle were part of the Northumberland area, the largest, which at this stage had an allocation of over 350 vehicles. However, vehicles from the Durham and Tees-side areas also appeared on the various longer-distance stage carriage services from County Durham and points further south. In addition Yorkshire area vehicles could also be seen from time to time. On 5th December 1970 this Durham area 1956 Bristol LS6B with 39-seat ECW bodywork was photographed at Marlborough Crescent bus station. Fleet No. 2310 (10 BHN) was awaiting time to depart for Bishop Auckland on service 56 operated jointly with Northern General.

United No. 6002 (LHN 265D) was a 1966 Bristol RELL with ECW 50-seat bodywork in stage/express livery. It was photographed on 10th April 1971 leaving Marlborough Crescent bus station on service X30 to Ashington. This joint service with Northern General between Ashington, Newcastle, Stanley and Lanchester had been created by linking the two operators' previously separate services across Newcastle which produced a number of new links not previously possible without a change of bus. The Bristol RELL depicted on the previous page originally had the same type of body as fleet No. 6002.

Service 515 was a lengthy stage carriage service between Glasgow, Peebles, Galashiels, Jedburgh, Newcastle and Whitley Bay operated jointly by United and Eastern Scottish. On 15th August 1971 this United Bristol MW6G with ECW 39-seat bodywork was seen arriving at Haymarket bus station after its seven-hour journey from Glasgow. The green and cream colouring was the long-established express/coach livery used by United which originated with the acquisition in 1934 of the business of Orange Brothers of Bedlington which operated long-distance services from the North East to London.

This picture, taken on 21st March 1971 at Haymarket bus station parking area, shows Eastern Scottish fleet No. ZA181 (EWS 181D) a 1966 Alexander-bodied Bristol RELH which had arrived on service 508 from Edinburgh. This service was the least frequent of three separate stage carriage services between Edinburgh and Newcastle operated jointly by United and Eastern Scottish. The 1970/71 winter timetable provided only one daily return journey leaving Edinburgh at 0855 hours and returning from Newcastle at 1645 hours. The journey time was about five hours. The most frequent timetable was provided by services 504-6 via the A1 (Great North Road) and a lower frequency was provided on service 510 via Kelso and Wooler.

This picture, taken on 7th February 1973, shows United 455 (AHN 155B) a 1964 Bristol FLF 6B with ECW bodywork at Barras Bridge approaching St. Mary's Place from Blyth on service 408. This route was then operated jointly with Tynemouth and District Transport on the section of route between Newcastle and Whitley Bay. The traditional United livery on this bus was soon to be superseded by NBC red livery.

United was an early user of the ECW-bodied Bristol VR and it took delivery of batches of this model throughout its availability. Fleet No. 691 (SUP 691R) was photographed at Haymarket on 22nd September 1976 when still new. It was in standard NBC red livery. Service 405 was one of a busy group of routes provided between Blyth, Cramlington new town and Newcastle.

United No. 1520 (AHN 320H) was one of the earlier ECW-bodied Bristol LH saloons in this fleet. It was photographed on 20th September 1978 near Marlborough Crescent bus station before returning to Morpeth on a service which gave a link south of Haymarket bus station, the usual terminus for routes from Morpeth. It is being overtaken by Northern General No. 4383 (YUP 577F) a former Venture Transport Leyland Leopard.

Above:

By 1980 United vehicles used on services wholly within Tyne and Wear were appearing in full yellow and white livery as used on PTE vehicles. Fleet No. 817 (APT 817W) is pictured leaving Marlborough Crescent bus station for Heddon-on-the-Wall on 31st August 1980. This service later transferred to the PTE as part of the reallocation of bus services following Metro introduction.

Left:

United No. 4229 (BHN 429H) an ECW bodied Bristol RELL, was photographed in full Tyne and Wear yellow livery on 12th August 1981 having just departed Eldon Square bus station for North Shields on service 355. This service operated through areas of North Tyneside served by the Metro system and as a consequence was diverted at the time Metro was introduced to serve Four Lane Ends Metro interchange.

By the early 1980s the United fleet included many dual-purpose Leyland Leopards, some of which were acquired second-hand. Fleet No. 6062 (GGR 406N) was a former Northern General Plaxton-bodied Leyland Leopard which United acquired in 1982. It was photographed on 22nd April 1984 passing Gallowgate coach station having just left Eldon Square bus station on service 685 bound for Carlisle. The Carlisle service had been given a new route number in 1973 and had moved its terminus to the new Eldon Square bus station in 1982.

At the beginning of 1970 Venture Transport was operating a modern fleet of 85 vehicles on services within north-west County Durham including several key routes into Newcastle's Marlborough Crescent bus station. The fleet was all single-deck because of the many low bridges in the areas it served, but consideration was being given to the scope for using double-deckers. However, on 30th April 1970 Venture Transport was acquired by Northern General and although it was initially retained as a separate subsidiary, it was completely absorbed by the end of 1974. This photograph, taken just before the takeover in 1970, shows fleet No. 290 (HUP 390H) an Alexander-bodied Leyland Leopard. This was numerically the last of the final batch of six vehicles delivered to Venture as an independent company. It was photographed at Allendale, near Consett, on the route of services 5 and 12 between Newcastle, Rowlands Gill, Medomsley and Consett.

By the date of this photograph, taken on 2nd September 1981, OK Motor Services had moved the terminus of its hourly Bishop Auckland-Newcastle service from Marlborough Crescent bus station to a new bus stand in Newgate Street adjacent to the Eldon Square shopping development. This 10-metre 1974 Leyland Atlantean (GGR 103N) with 83-seat Northern Counties bodywork is seen loading prior to departure on the 75-minute journey to Bishop Auckland. The vehicle is painted in the later version of the traditional livery which was soon to be modified.

Wright Brothers commenced their Newcastle, Hexham, Alston, Penrith, Keswick service in 1926 and this lengthy stage carriage route is characterised by the spectacular scenery as it crosses the wild north Pennines. This picture, taken at Marlborough Crescent bus station on 26th April 1972, shows Wright Brothers Bedford VAM with Plaxton Derwent bodywork (VRM 100H) awaiting its time to depart for Alston.

In the 1970s and 1980s T. B. Vasey continued to provide the Otterburn to Newcastle service. This very rural route, over 30 miles in length, had three or four trips a day provided by Vasey. In addition infrequent United/Eastern Scottish stage services between Edinburgh or Glasgow and Newcastle provided two or three journeys a day via Otterburn. This picture, taken in October 1975 shows Vasey's new Duple-bodied Bedford YRT (KCN 313P) leaving Haymarket bus station bound for Otterburn via Ponteland.

Robert Tindall Coaches (Tyneside) Ltd trading as Low Fell Coaches had originated as a taxi and minibus operator in the late 1950s but achieved great publicity in 1983 when it was granted a licence to operate a 'Cross Tyne Service' between Low Fell, Gateshead and Newcastle. This followed the truncation of many local bus services from the Gateshead area at Gateshead Metro interchange in 1981. This photograph, taken on 23rd June 1984, shows former London Country Bus Services Plaxton-bodied AEC Reliance (TPD 22S) laying over near Eldon Square bus station prior to departing from St. Thomas' Street for Low Fell.

PART THREE
1986-1996

Busways Travel Services was the company formed to take over the PTE's bus operations from 26th October 1986. A new feature was the introduction of minibuses with the Mini Busways fleetname. Also new was the MetroCentre Shuttle service 100 between Newcastle city centre and the new and expanding MetroCentre shopping development in Gateshead. On 14th March 1987 fleet No. 1404 (D404 DFT), a new Mercedes Benz 709D with Reebur body conversion, was seen picking up passengers at Newcastle central station. By 1989 this route had been converted to single-deck bus allocation as traffic continued to grow.

Busways had a need for extra vehicles as a consequence of early tendering success and part of this need was met by eleven former Lancashire United Plaxton-bodied Leyland Leopards purchased from Greater Manchester Buses. This picture, taken on 25th July 1987, shows City Busways No. 1846 (MTE 15R) in Percy Street proceeding towards Central Station. The Killingworth Express service had been re-introduced at the time of deregulation, restoring this facility between Killingworth new town and the city which had been previously replaced by a connecting facility at Four Lane Ends Metro interchange when Metro was introduced.

Sixty-five Alexander-bodied Leyland Olympians were delivered to the PTE in 1985 and these were the newest buses in the Busways fleet when the company was formed. The distinctive yellow colour had been a feature of Newcastle's public transport for over 60 years and Busways continued with the yellow and white livery and added a third colour dependent upon the operating division. In Newcastle, there were two Busways divisions – City Busways and Newcastle Busways – based on Byker and Slatyford Lane depots respectively and they used the same livery with maroon as the third colour. Fleet No. 611 (C611 LFT) was seen on 6th April 1988 in Grainger Street proceeding west-bound to Throckley on service 21.

Busways purchased 27 Leyland Lynx saloons and for a period six of these were allocated to City Busways. This photograph, taken on 16th April 1989, shows fleet No. 123 (F123 HVK) operating west-bound past Gallowgate coach station on service 12 to Two Ball Lonnen, Fenham. This cross-city route was one of the company's busiest services and was one of the earliest motor bus routes wholly within the city, having originated in 1929. Busways became a privatised company on 5th May 1989 when it was purchased by its senior management and employees from Tyne and Wear Passenger Transport Authority.

Busways purchased 70 9.8-metre Dennis Darts between 1992 and 1994 and they were allocated to all bus operating divisions of the company. Bodywork was by Alexander (47) and Plaxton (23). City Busways No. 1705 (K705 PCN), an Alexander-bodied example, was photographed on 28th December 1992 in Blackett Street operating to Wallsend on service 40B. The route was a variation of the frequent service 40 and had been introduced at the time of intense competition with Welcome Passenger Services in Newcastle.

In 1991 Busways took an opportunity to up-date its fleet by acquiring 21 1987 Northern Counties-bodied Leyland Olympians from Bexleybus, part of London Buses, which had found them redundant after losing contracts. These vehicles were in fact part of a cancelled Greater Manchester Buses order. City Busways fleet No. 689 (E918 KYR) was photographed on 26th June 1991 leaving Blackett Street on service 40 bound for Lemington Road End.

Busways followed a dual-sourcing policy for its new vehicles and in 1994 took delivery of ten new single-deckers for evaluation. These included Dennis, Scania and Volvo types with Alexander, Northern Counties, Optare and Plaxton bodies. Fleet No. 953 (M953 DRG) is a Scania L113 with Alexander Strider bodywork. It was photographed in Blackett Street on 22nd April 1996 operating westbound to Chapel House on service 12A and displaying its newly acquired Stagecoach Busways livery.

Busways had a third operating division in the Newcastle area – Blue Bus Services. This was established in 1986 to operate the company's services into Northumberland and was subsequently developed as a low cost division to operate other lower revenue services commercially and to bid for contracts. The initial fleet included a number of Duple-bodied Leyland Leopards transferred from coaching duties. Blue Bus Services No. 1891 (GBB 991N) was photographed on 14th September 1986 passing Gallowgate coach station having just left Eldon Square bus station on service 76 for Ponteland village and Darras Hall.

Blue Bus Services became a significant operator of Bristol RE vehicles and by 1995 operated sixteen examples with a further dozen held in storage or partially cannibalised. Fleet No. 1817 (JMW 166P) was a former Thamesdown Transport vehicle dating from 1975. It was photographed in March 1990 at Stamfordham village having just arrived from Newcastle on Service 74.

The first brand new vehicles for Blue Bus Services were two Reeve Burgess (Plaxton)-bodied Dennis Darts delivered in 1992. These were followed by three more in 1993 to enable the Newcastle, Ponteland village, Darras Hall service to be so equipped. Fleet No. 1702 (J702 KCU) was photographed in Percy Street on 27th May 1992 having just departed from Eldon Square bus station on service 75 bound for Darras Hall via Kingston Park.

The Tyne & Wear Omnibus Company (TWOC) was formed in 1987 and operated services in Newcastle and Sunderland, mainly in competition with Busways, between 1987 and 1989. It was in the same ownership as the long-established Trimdon Motor Services in County Durham and its fleet was presented in a similar white and blue livery. The bulk of the fleet was made up of ECW-bodied Bristol LH saloons but there were also some Leyland Leopards. One of the more unusual Bristols was this Marshall-bodied LHS (VOD 123K) which was acquired from Southern National. It was photographed on 14th May 1988 at Gallowgate operating east-bound to Walker competing with Busways service 12. The 88-vehicle TWOC business was sold to Go Ahead Northern in November 1989 and resold on the same day to Busways.

In 1991 Busways experienced further significant competition on a number of its busiest services from the newly-established Welcome Passenger Services which commenced with a fleet of 21 minibuses and subsequently increased its fleet to 38 such vehicles. The fleet included sixteen Renault S75 minibuses with Plaxton Beaver bodywork. One of these (J230 JJR) was photographed on 27th May 1992 leaving Blackett Street on service 400 to Chapel House which competed with Busways service 40 via Stanhope Street and the West Road to Lemington Road End.

In preparation for the introduction of deregulation Northern General re-launched itself with a new image as Go Ahead Northern and rapid steps were taken to present the fleet in the brighter red and white livery. On 7th May 1987 the company was purchased by its senior management from the National Bus Company. This picture, taken on 28th February 1988, shows MCW Metrobus No. 3758 (C758 OCN) passing Gallowgate coach station having just left Eldon Square bus station on service 610 bound for Chopwell.

The Go Ahead Northern livery is well illustrated by this picture, taken on 29th March 1989, of Bristol VRT No. 3342 (UTO 833S). This was one of several vehicles diverted to Northern General from a Trent order in 1978. The bus was photographed in Newgate Street proceeding towards Eldon Square bus station on service X95 from Parkside and Sunderland.

VFM Buses is the trading name of Go Ahead Group subsidiary The Tyneside Omnibus Co Ltd which is based at South Shields. VFM Buses operate the successful service X23 between Sunderland and Newcastle – the Two Cities Express. VFM fleet No. 5117 (A717 ABB), a Plaxton-bodied Leyland Tiger, was photographed in Blackett Street on 28th December 1992 whilst loading passengers prior to departure on service X23. Most of the activities of VFM Buses are local services in the South Shields, Jarrow and Hebburn areas including routes feeding into Heworth Metro interchange for passengers wishing to join the Metro for Newcastle.

Go Ahead Group subsidiary The Gateshead & District Omnibus Co Ltd trades as Go Ahead Gateshead. It provides many services into Newcastle. On 28th December 1992 fleet No. 3676 (G676 TCN), an Alexander-bodied Leyland Olympian, was taking on passengers at Newgate Street bus stand prior to departure for Sunnside on service 644.

The Sunderland & District Omnibus Co Ltd trading as Wear Buses is the Go Ahead Group subsidiary based on Sunderland area which provides a number of longer distance services into Newcastle. MCW Metrobus No. 3501 (UTN 501Y) was photographed on 28th April 1993 in Newgate Street, having just left Eldon Square bus station, bound for Washington new town and Sunderland on service X4. Wear Buses has steadily developed limited-stop services into Newcastle from various parts of Wearside and east County Durham.

Coastline Buses is the trading name of The Tynemouth & District Omnibus Co Ltd, the Go Ahead Group subsidiary serving the North Tyneside area. This Wright-bodied Dennis Dart, fleet No. 8086 (K986 SCU), was photographed on 21st April 1993 bound for North Shields via Battle Hill on service 300. This picture was taken in Haymarket and the bus had just left Eldon Square bus station, the terminal then used by most Coastline services into Newcastle.

The Northern General Transport Co Ltd is the Go Ahead Group subsidiary which continued operations from Consett, Stenley and Chester-le-Street garages. Consett garage was closed in 1994. Northern operates a considerable number of medium and longer-distance services from County Durham into Newcastle. This 1984 MCW Metrobus displays the latest version of the Northern livery. Fleet No. 3625 (A625 BCN) was photographed on 24th April 1996 at Haymarket proceeding towards Eldon Square bus station for departure on service 735 to Houghton-le-Spring. This service had been operated to and from Worswick Street bus station until 1st April 1996 but this long-established bus station was then closed. From the next day its services were mainly transferred to Eldon Square bus station which was itself reorganised to coincide with the opening of the redeveloped Haymarket bus station.

From time to time Go Ahead Northern subsidiaries adopted non-standard identities when in specific competitive situations. On 28th April 1993 Go Ahead Gateshead was operating Plaxton-bodied Leyland Tiger No. 7026 (JSK 327) seen here loading at Newgate Street bus stand. Services B & C operated in competition with a service provided by Classic Buses in the south-west Gateshead area.

Low Fell Coaches was acquired by Go Ahead Northern in June 1992 and continued to provide its 'Cross Tyne Service' between Low Fell, Gateshead and Newcastle. On 23rd February 1994 this new Plaxton-bodied Dennis Lance (L141 YTY) was photographed in St. Thomas' Street awaiting departure for Gateshead and Low Fell.

As its expansion continued OK Motor Services adopted the trading name OK Travel and a revised fleet livery. This 10-metre Northern Counties-bodied Leyland Olympian entered service in 1989, one of a batch of three. It was photographed on 12th July 1989 arriving at Newgate Street from Bishop Auckland. OK Travel continued its expansion between 1989 and March 1995 when it was acquired by the Go Ahead Group. The fleet totalled 225 vehicles at this time.

Northumbria Motor Services was formed from the Northumberland area of United Automobile Services and commenced operations in September 1986. On 21st October 1987 it was purchased by its senior management from the National Bus Company. From formation Northumbria adopted a distinctive red, grey and white livery. Fleet No. 717 (GOL 421N) was a former Midland Red North Leyland National. It was photographed on 25th July 1987 in Percy Street on service 46 bound for Whitley Bay.

Northumbria's first new double-deckers were 10-metre Leyland Olympians with coach-seated Alexander bodies delivered in 1988. This batch of ten vehicles has been mainly employed on medium distance limited-stop services from south-east Northumberland into Newcastle. In this picture, taken on 12th July 1989, fleet No. 305 (F305 JTY) is seen arriving at Haymarket bus station on service X23 from Blyth via Cramlington new town.

Right: Northumbria purchased second-hand a number of 10-metre Leyland Olympians with an express version of the ECW body. One of those acquired from associated company Kentish Bus was damaged by fire and it was rebodied by Northern Counties in 1992. This vehicle was fleet No. 353 (A103 FPL) which was photographed on 9th August 1992 in St. Mary's Place proceeding towards Eldon Square bus station on service 306 from Tynemouth.

Below left: H. W. Hunter & Sons of Seaton Delaval, Northumberland commenced operations in 1929 and until deregulation the main activity was a service between North Shields, Whitley Bay and Seaton Delaval. Following deregulation the company expanded in the North Tyneside area and the business was sold to British Bus at the same time as Northumbria in 1994. Hunter's is now part of Northumbria and operates the former Moor Dale bus services as well as their existing routes. An interesting development from 30th July 1995 was the extension of services 365/6 (Cramlington-Freeman Hospital) into central Newcastle in competition with Busways service 38. This photograph taken on 24th April 1996 shows Hunter's Fleet No. 74 (K74 SRG) a former Moor Dale Plaxton-bodied Dennis Dart leaving the new Haymarket bus station for Cramlington.

Below right: After an early batch of sixteen-seat Freight Rover Sherpas, Northumbria standardised on the MCW and Optare Metrorider for its minibus requirements. Number 853 (K853 RBB) was a 28-seat version delivered in 1992. It was pictured on 21st April 1993 in Barras Bridge near to Eldon Square bus station on its journey from North Tyneside on service 355.

Ribble ceased being joint operator with United of the Newcastle-Carlisle service in February 1986 when its Carlisle operations were transferred to Cumberland Motor Services in preparation for deregulation and privatisation. In addition United ceased its involvement in the service with the formation of Northumbria later in 1986. Cumberland was acquired by Stagecoach in July 1987 and this photograph, taken on 24th May 1989, shows Cumberland No. 612 (GLS 267S) passing Gallowgate coach station having just departed Eldon Square bus station for Carlisle. This Alexander-bodied Leyland Leopard had been acquired from Kelvin Scottish in 1987.

Cumberland No. 784 (K784 DAO) was photographed on 29th September 1993 in Percy Street having just left Eldon Square bus station for Carlisle on service 685. Stagecoach placed 90 of these Alexander-bodied Volvo B10M saloons in service with Cumberland in 1992/93 to significantly upgrade the fleet. Fleet No. 784 was one of seventeen vehicles with 48 coach-type seats delivered in 1993.

Above: United Automobile Services Ltd is part of North East Bus Ltd which is a subsidiary of National Express-owned West Midlands Travel. North East Bus also includes Tees & District Transport and Teesside Motor Services and the main areas of activity are County Durham, Cleveland and parts of North Yorkshire. However, United and Tees & District both operate into Newcastle on a number of longer-distance services, some of which are jointly operated with Northern General Transport. This Alexander-bodied Leyland Olympian was photographed on 22nd April 1996 arriving at Eldon Square bus station from Darlington and Durham on service 723. Fleet No. 272 (L272 FVN) was new in 1994.

Right: Tees & District Transport operates into Eldon Square bus station on services X1 and X10 from Middlesbrough which are jointly operated with United and Northern. Fleet No. 243 (A563 KWY) was photographed leaving Eldon Square bus station on 23rd April 1996. This ECW-bodied Leyland Olympian joined the Tees & District fleet from West Riding in 1994.

Hylton Castle Coaches commenced operations in the 1950s with the fleet being employed on private hires, excursions and contracts. At deregulation it introduced the fleet name Catch A Bus and launched local services in the South Shields area and these have been progressively developed. The company also introduced its service 3 between South Shields and Newcastle and this picture of a Willowbrook-bodied Leyland Leopard (VFA 69X) was taken in Percy Street on 24th January 1987. The service was soon withdrawn, probably because it could not attract sufficient traffic from the Metro service between South Shields and Newcastle. By April 1996, however, a new service 15 had been introduced between South Shields area and Newcastle.

Rochester and Marshall was formed in 1951 and acquired various rural services in the Hexham area and expansion followed in the 1960s. This Bedford YLQ with Plaxton bodywork (BBB 548V) was photographed on 25th March 1987 passing Gallowgate coach station having just left Newgate Street bound for Ponteland, Stamfordham and Matfen on service 879. Rochester & Marshall by this stage was part of the Moor Dale coach group which was acquired subsequently by Proudmutual, the owners of Northumbria. This version of service 879 had been introduced at the time of deregulation and produced competition with Blue Bus Services route 74 between Newgate Street and Matfen which in itself was successor to R. Armstrong's service which Busways predecessor the PTE had acquired in 1973.

A number of former Northern General employees set up North Eastern Bus Services just prior to deregulation and they gained a number of Tyne and Wear PTE service contracts. This picture, taken at Marlborough Crescent bus station on 24th May 1987, shows an Alexander-bodied Leyland Leopard (LHL 248P) which was new to Yorkshire Traction. This business ceased trading in March 1989.

T. B. Vasey continued the Newcastle-Otterburn service after deregulation and in addition, for a while, competed with Blue Bus Services between Eldon Square bus station and Ponteland village. Vasey usually used two Mercedes minibuses on this operation. On 29th March 1989 Mercedes 609D (E420 YLG) was photographed leaving Eldon Square bus station for Ponteland. The service was withdrawn in January 1990.

Left: ERB Services was formed in November 1986 and by 1995 operated nine minibuses. ERB operates former Busways service 6 between the Central Station and Jesmond Vale which it took over after a successful tender bid. ERB now operates the service commercially. On 25th July 1990 Ford Transit/ Dormobile minibus (D550 VVV) was photographed in Grainger Street approaching its Central Station terminus.

Below left: H. J. Snaith of Otterburn acquired services in the Otterburn area from M. Reed in 1975. In October 1986 journeys were introduced between Otterburn and Newcastle partially replacing journeys previously provided by T. B. Vasey. Snaith provides several journeys on weekdays and in 1995 Blue Bus Services withdrew its daily return journey from Otterburn where it had a bus out-stationed. This Ford Transit (F481 HPP) was photographed on 12th September 1990 leaving Eldon Square bus station for Otterburn.

Below right: Amberline Motor Services of Whitley Bay operates a half-hourly minibus service from the Whitley Bay area to Newcastle on Mondays to Saturdays. This photograph taken on 28th December 1992, shows Amberline's Robin Hood-bodied Iveco (C511 DYM) which was new to London Buses in 1985. The bus was loading in Blackett Street for Whitley Bay. Amberline had been known as A1 Taxis until 1992 and its service was developed from a withdrawn Northumbria operation.

T. & A. Anderson of Westerhope was established by the time of the Second World War as a contract and private hire operator. It entered local service operation on tendered services after deregulation. In addition, by the late 1980s, a number of commercial services were introduced in competition with Busways services between the Westerhope area and the city centre. In 1991 this Alexander-bodied Seddon Pennine (RCS 710R) was photographed in Newgate Street awaiting departure for Westerhope and Chapel House. T. & A. Anderson ceased trading in August 1992.

Classic Coaches of Annfield Plain, County Durham commenced local services in 1992 and has grown to a fleet of over 40 coaches and buses. Its commercial and tendered local services have been mainly developed as a result of active competition with the Go Ahead Group. In July 1994 this Leyland National (PTT 89R) was seen at Beamish Museum bound for Worswick Street bus station on service 709 from Stanley. This particular journey was a Durham County Council tendered operation although the main part of this service was provided commercially by Go Ahead subsidiary Northern.

Left: North Rider provides mainly tendered services for Tyne and Wear PTE having been established in April 1991. On 29th October 1995 North Rider's former Badgerline ECW-bodied Bristol RELL (LHT 171L) was seen at Newcastle Central Station awaiting departure on a special operation.

Below left: Redby was formed in the 1950s and prior to 1986 was involved with private hire and contract operations. Following deregulation local services were developed in the Sunderland area. Services have also operated into Newcastle more recently and on 10th April 1995 service X97 was introduced between Silksworth, Sunderland and Eldon Square bus station. This Marshall-bodied Volvo B6 (L84 CNY) was photographed at Eldon Square bus station on 24th April 1996.

Below: Stagecoach Darlington was established by Busways in November 1994 and by 1995 it became part of Stagecoach-owned Cleveland Transit. Stagecoach Darlington substantially replaced the services of municipally-owned Darlington Transport Company including an express service between Darlington, Newton Aycliffe, MetroCentre and Newcastle. This Alexander-bodied Volvo B10M, fleet No. 552 (N552 VDC) was photographed approaching Eldon Square bus station on service X90 from Darlington on 23rd April 1996.